MY FIRST REFERENCE LIBRARY

EXPLORERS

by Julie Brown and Robert Brown
Adapted from John Man's
Exploration and Discovery

BELITHA PRESS

First published in Great Britain in 1990 by
Belitha Press Limited
31 Newington Green, London N16 9PU

ISBN 1 85561 039 6
Reprinted 1991, 1992
Printed in Hong Kong for Imago

British Library Cataloguing in Publication Data
CIP data for this book is available from the British Library

Acknowledgements

Photographic credits:

Bryan and Cherry Alexander 25 bottom
The Bodleian Library 24
Christian Bonington 59 top
Bridgeman Art Library 21 top
John Cleare/Mountain Camera 9, 13 top, 32/33, 49 left, 51, 54 right, 55 centre
ET Archive 22, 23, 25 top left and right, 50 right
Mary Evans Picture Library 53 bottom, 54 left
Derek Fordham/Arctic Camera 57
Werner Forman Archive 15 bottom
Giraudon 27
Susan Griggs/Leon Schadeberg 6, /Victor Englebert 41 top, /Robert Azzi 46, /Anthony Howarth 47 top
Sonia Halliday 6 bottom
Robert Harding Picture Library 17, /George Douglass Brewerton: Crossing the Rocky Mountains, in the collection of The Corcoran Gallery of Art, Gift of William Wilson Corcoran 29, /Schloss Tegel, East Berlin 37 top, 44, 53 top
Michael Holford 14 left, 18 right, 35 top
Hulton Picture Company 21 bottom, 30, 37 bottom, 45 bottom
Hutchison Library 31 top, 41 bottom, 43
MacDonald/Aldus Archive 39, 42, 45 top
Magnum 32
Mansell Collection 33, 40, 50 left
Marion and Tony Morrison 34, 35 bottom, 36, 38
National Maritime Museum 14 right
Oxford Scientific Films 13 bottom, 19, 31 bottom
Photo Library of Australia 49 top
Popperfoto 47 bottom
Rapho 5
Ronan Picture Library 18 left
Science Photo Library 58
Frank Spooner Pictures 59 centre
Charles Swithinbank 55 top
Viking Museum, Oslo 10

Maps by: Lovell Johns Ltd
Illustrated by: Nick Shewring (Garden Studios), Eugene Fleury

Series editors: Neil Champion and Mark Sachner
Educational consultant: Carolyn Kain
Editors: Kate Scarborough and Rita Reitci
Designed by: Groom and Pickerill
Picture research: Ann Usborne

Contents

Words found in **bold** are explained in the glossary on pages 60 and 61

CHAPTER ONE

WHY EXPLORE?

Early Explorers

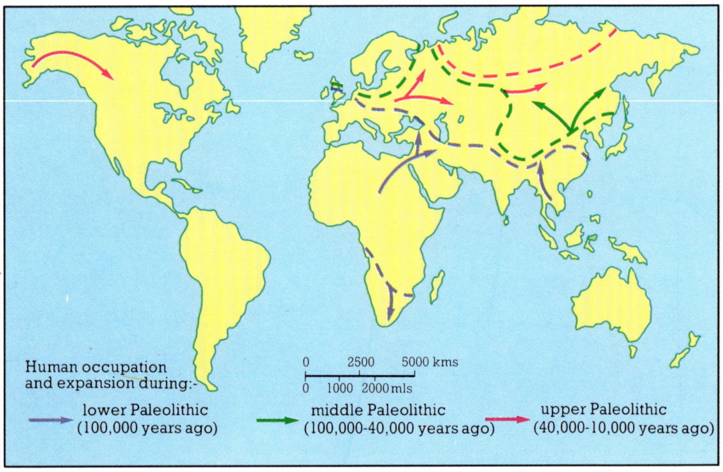

► This map shows how early people spread across the Earth (100,000 to 10,000 years ago).

▲ A group of Stone Age people, near the end of the last ice age (11,000 years ago).

What is Exploration?

About one million years ago some humans moved from regions of Africa to the cooler parts of the world. By the end of the last ice age, 11,000 years ago, people had spread to every **continent** except Antarctica. These early humans moved around, looking for better places to live. Explorers are different. They explore to find places to trade with, to steal, to learn, to become famous, to settle, or to spread religion. But all explorers have one thing in common. They want to bring or send knowledge of unknown places back to their homelands.

Growing nations

Explorers usually came from wealthy, growing nations. Some explorers were traders who wanted valuable metals, spices, or gems. While others were interested in what was beyond the horizon, or they were scholars who wanted to know more about other peoples, places, and ideas. Most of these explorers took great risks and found their journeys very difficult.

▲ These paintings of bison are on the walls of caves in Lascaux, France. The pictures are about 30,000 years old, made by people known as the Cro-Magnons.

▼ The people below lived for thousands of years before they first met with white European explorers.

Starting to Explore

▼ Mediterranean shores were once clean like this.

Did you know?

► The Phoenicians were some of the first explorers to leave the Mediterranean. They lived in what is now Israel and Lebanon. They were skilled seamen.

CHAPTER TWO

THE ANCIENT WORLD

The Mediterranean Sea is 4,000 km (2,500 miles) long. It has warm, calm waters and many safe harbours. For hundreds of years, no one living there knew what lay beyond its shores.

Navigation

Early sailors steered by wind direction, stars, currents, and the

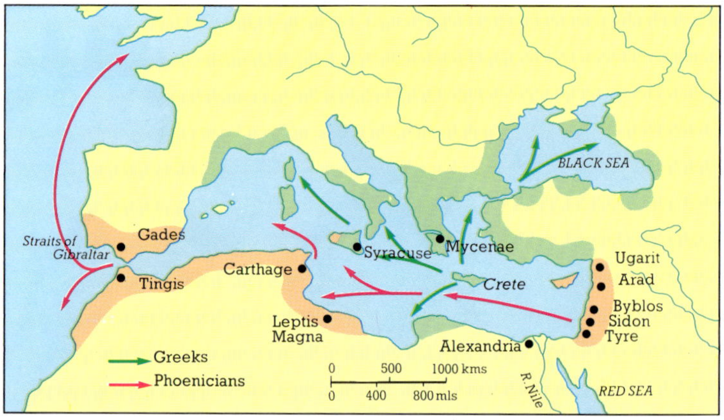

► Carthage, in Tunisia, is now a ruin in the desert. When the Phoenicians built it in 800 BC, it was a port in a fertile land.

shape of the land. They had no **compasses** and sometimes got lost when clouds covered the stars and the Sun.

The ancient Egyptians

In 2,600 BC, the Egyptians made the first seagoing voyage ever written down. Egypt was the greatest early civilization of the Mediterranean. In about 600 BC, the **pharaoh** of Egypt, Necho, started trading with Arabia and East Africa. This trade was over land and very slow. So Necho paid a Phoenician **fleet** to find a sea route around Africa. The Phoenicians did, but it took them three years – far too long to use as a trade route.

▲ Ancient Greek stories tell of a great explorer called Ulysses. The journey he took from Troy to Ithaca was described by the Greek poet, Homer, about 2,500 years ago.

Did you know?

Hanno was a Phoenician from Carthage. He left with 60 ships to reach and settle on the west coast of Africa. On his trip, he saw 'women with hairy bodies' – probably chimpanzees. 'We caught three women, who bit and scratched', he wrote.

The Greeks

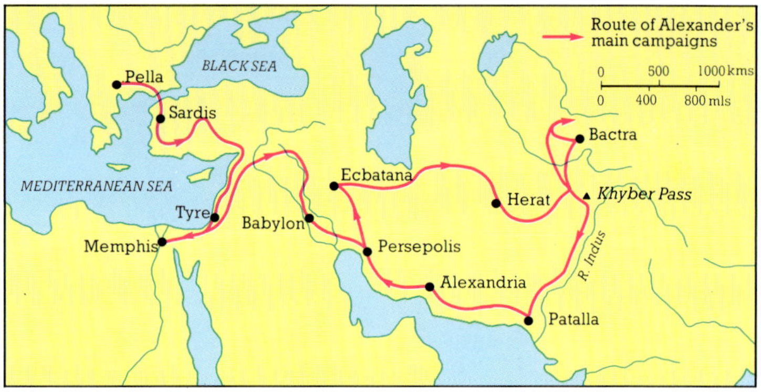

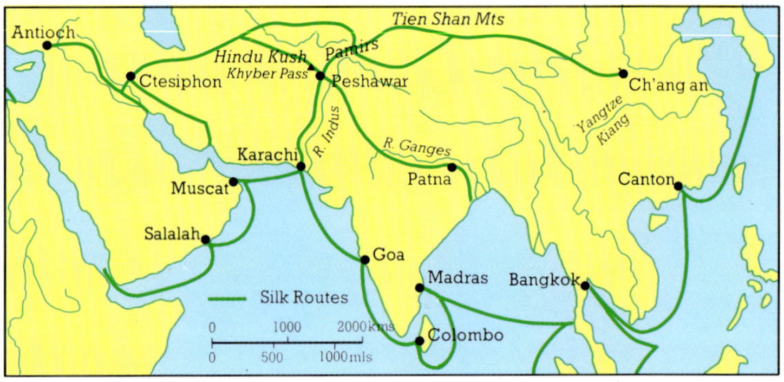

► (Top) Alexander the Great led his conquering army along this route. (Bottom) This map shows the ancient silk trade route across Asia.

▼ Alexander the Great, one of the world's greatest travellers.

The Greeks were the greatest explorers of the ancient world. They set up over 100 **colonies** around the Mediterranean and the Black Sea. About 400 BC, the Greeks began to look beyond the Mediterranean Sea.

Alexander the Great

At the age of 23, Alexander was king of Macedonia – at the time, not part of Greece. He wanted to conquer the whole world, but he had no way of knowing how big it was. In 334 BC, he led his army eastward to conquer Persia – now

Iran – and planned to go on to India. Alexander reached Afghanistan, marched through the Khyber Pass, and went down the Indus river. But he died of a fever at the age of 33, in Babylon, near present-day Baghdad, Iraq.

Exploring the north

Very few Greeks went to explore the damp, cold lands of northern Europe. One of the first to do so was Pytheas. He sailed to England and found out it was an island. He then went farther north to a land he called Thule. Today, we are not sure where Thule is, but it may have been in Norway or Iceland.

The Silk Road

The Chinese wanted to make links with the west, so they could sell silk to the rich people of Europe. No one in Europe knew how to make silk. The Chinese explorer, Chang Chi'en, opened trade routes to the west. Between 138 BC and 126 BC, Chang Chi'en explored the Tien Shan mountains, Pamirs, and Hindu Kush as far west as the Khyber Pass. In AD 399 a Buddhist monk, Fa Hsien, made a 15 year journey as far as Sri Lanka.

▼ Part of the Silk Road in Kirgizia, in southern Soviet Union.

CHAPTER THREE

GROWING NATIONS

The Vikings

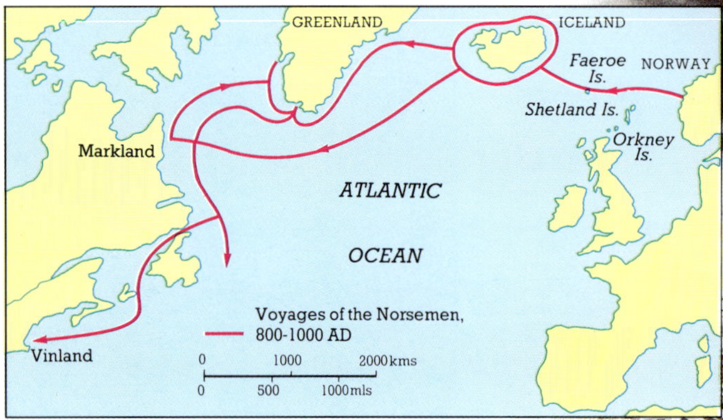

▲ This map shows the routes Vikings took to Vinland in longboats like this one. ▼

Around AD 1000, a brave group of sailors, the Vikings, explored the icy waters of the North Atlantic Ocean. They sailed in sturdy wooden ships called knorrs that held up to 30 people, with food and cattle.

East and west

The Vikings ventured from their home in Scandinavia as far east as Constantinople, which they reached in AD 860. On the way, they went through Russia,

Did you know?

The Vikings, expert sailors, used the wind, the Sun, birds, currents, water colour, ice and fog to navigate.

moving their ships over land from river to river. About the same time, the Vikings also travelled west to Iceland. One Icelander, Eric the Red, discovered Greenland in AD 982. Many Vikings lived there until the climate became too cold.

Discovering Vinland

About AD 1000, Eric's son, Leif the Lucky, sailed farther west to a warmer, wooded area that he called Vinland. It was in North America. Leif and his men spent a winter there. Two other expeditions followed this one. But the native Indians who lived there attacked the Vikings, making it impossible for them to settle.

St Brendan in his currach

Saint Brendan, the Explorer

Saint Brendan may have been the first explorer to cross the Atlantic. After Christianity came to Ireland in AD 432, Irish monks travelled in open boats covered with animal hide, called currachs, looking for islands so they could live simply. Brendan was one of these monks. A book over 1,400 years old tells how Brendan sailed west and found 'crystal columns', that may have been icebergs, and 'a globe of fire', that may have been a volcano. The book also describes beautiful islands to the west, perhaps the Bahamas. No one knows for sure if the story is really true. A modern explorer, Tim Severin, actually sailed across the Atlantic in a currach.

◄ Vikings often stayed home in the winter. In the summer, they travelled great distances to trade or explore.

Going East

Arab explorers

The Arabs were also curious about the world. They travelled by land and sea. Arabs visited the countries of Denmark, England, China, and Russia. The greatest Arabian traveller was Ibn Battuta, from Morocco. In 1325, at the age of 22, Ibn left on a journey that lasted nearly 30 years and covered 120,000 km (75,000 miles)! He explored the Middle East, Russia, India, Africa, and China. Ibn wrote books about his adventures. In one, he described a giant bird, which he called a roc, that could carry away humans! No one knows if this is true however.

Europeans and Asians traded goods for many centuries until the **Mongols** began attacking Europe and the Near East in the 13th century. Then Genghis Khan, their leader, died. Europeans could then travel eastward again. The Pope sent friars – holy men – east to make friends with the Mongols. An Italian friar, John Carpini, was the first European to travel 4,800 km (3,000 miles) to the Mongol capital, in 1245. He wrote about his travels.

Marco Polo

Merchants soon followed the friars east. The most famous merchant traveller was Marco Polo. At the age of 17, he went east to China with his father and uncle. In 1275, the Polos arrived at the court of the **Great Khan**.

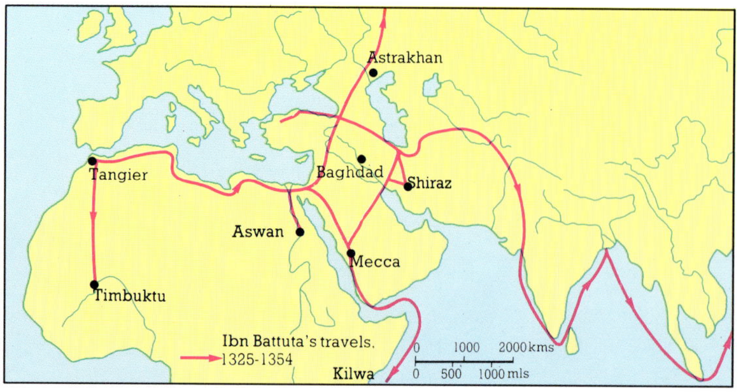

▶ The journeys of Ibn Battuta in the 1300s.

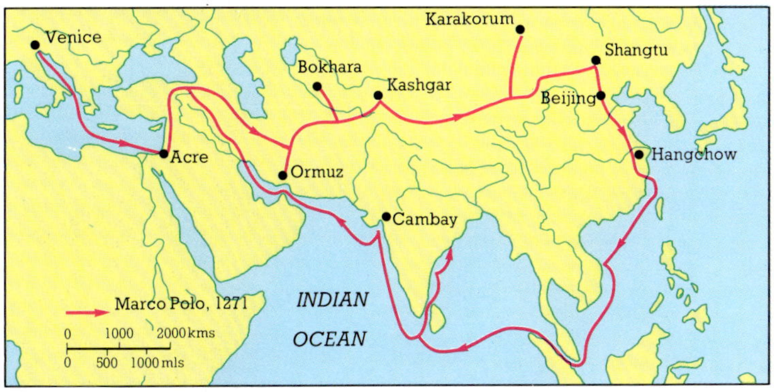

▲ The Great Wall of China – built around 300 BC to keep out invaders.

◀ The routes of Marco Polo's 21 years of travel in China and Asia.

They were impressed by the Khan's palace. The walls were gold and silver and the dining hall could seat 6,000 people! Marco kept a diary of all the things he saw on his travels. He saw a city with 12,000 bridges and he saw huge Chinese ships, called junks. After 21 years of travelling he returned home. For the next 50 years, Europeans freely travelled to the east, until **Muslim** nations would no longer allow them to pass through.

▲ The huge egg of the extinct elephant bird (left) is much bigger than an ostrich egg (centre left), a chicken's egg (centre right) and a tiny hummingbird's egg (right). Ibn Battuta's roc may have been based on the elephant bird.

Around Africa

The Phoenicians had journeyed around Africa for a long time. But most Europeans believed that Africa was a place of fire where rivers boiled.

Henry the Navigator

The Portuguese were the first Europeans to sail around Africa. In the 1440s Prince Henry the Navigator sent many ships out to explore. And in 1474 the first European ship crossed the **Equator**.

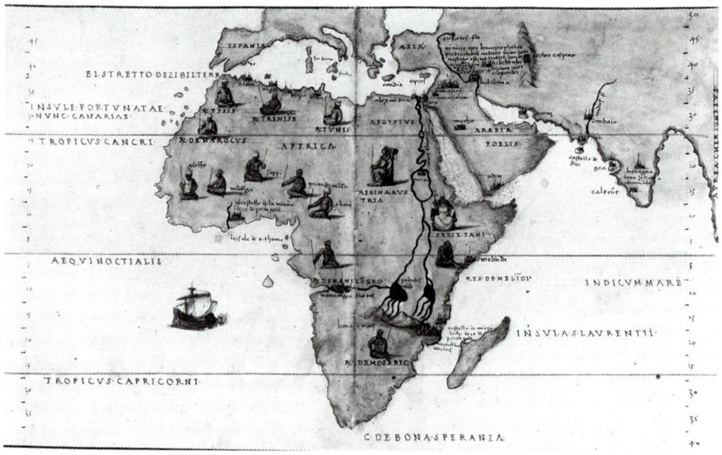

► This 17th-century map of Africa shows the correct coastline, but the interior was only guessed at.

▲ Prince Henry the Navigator paid for many voyages but did not go himself.

To India by sea

Two Portuguese explorers sailed south to find a trade route to India. One was Pedro da Covilhao, who landed on the coast of Ethiopia. He went no farther, and lived in Ethiopia for the rest of his life. The other was

Bartholomew Dias. In 1487 he sailed to the southern tip of Africa. The Portuguese king named the tip the Cape of Good Hope because he was hopeful that sailors could now sail all the way to India. Eleven years later, Vasco da Gama made the complete journey. It took two years. Merchants could now trade for precious spices without crossing through enemy countries.

▲ Chinese objects found on the island of Kilwa on the East African coast by Sir Mortimer Wheeler (above left). They show that China and Africa were trading along the silk routes. The picture below shows the ruins of a palace on Kilwa. Kilwa was at the centre of trading that took place along the East African coast. ▼

Columbus

Christopher Columbus knew that the world was round. He thought that he could reach India and the East quicker by sailing across the Atlantic Ocean, instead of all the way around Africa. He was misled by the maps of his day and the writings of Marco Polo. However, King Ferdinand and Queen Isabella of Spain thought such a journey was a good idea and might bring riches to Spain. They gave Columbus three ships and a hundred sailors for the voyage. In 1492, Columbus and his crew sailed westward into the unknown.

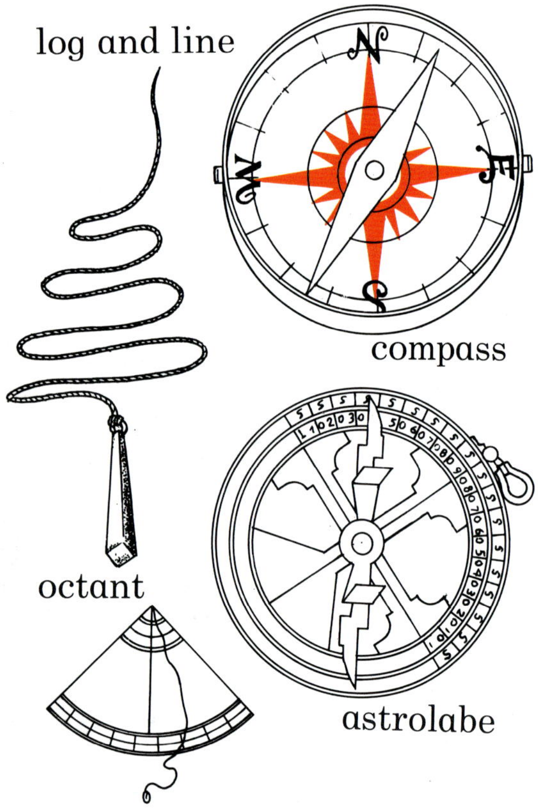

▲ Instruments used to navigate the seas.

► A cross-section view of Columbus's first ship, the *Santa Maria*. The sailors were cramped in small spaces.

The Bahamas

After two long months, just as the sailors were ready to **mutiny**, the lookout sighted land. Soon, friendly people swam out to greet the ship. Columbus called these native people Indians. He thought he was near India. He was really in the Bahamas.

Columbus crossed the Atlantic three more times, bringing Spaniards to start a colony. Columbus never found the riches of the East. But he did find a whole new world.

▲ The sight of land like this West Indian island must have cheered the sailors.

The naming of a continent

America took its name from an Italian called Amerigo Vespucci. His employers sent him to Spain to sell supplies to ships going to the New World. In Spain, he met Christopher Columbus. Vespucci later made voyages for Spain and for Portugal. He explored the coast of South America and was the first to describe it as a new continent. Martin Waldseemüller, a map maker, suggested either 'Amerige' or 'America' as the continent's name. Later, people began using the name for both North and South America.

Around the World

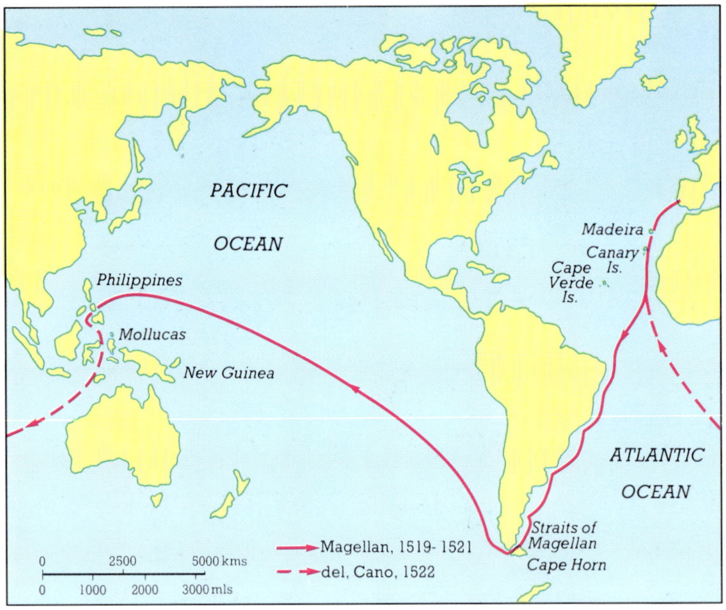

► The route of Magellan and del Cano, the captain who took over after Magellan's death.

▲ This portrait shows Magellan as a calm, dreamy man. He was also a tough sea captain.

After the discovery of the New World, Ferdinand Magellan, a Portuguese employed by Spain, promised to find a route to the Far East. Magellan set sail in 1519 with five ships and a crew of 237. It was a long and hard voyage. One ship was wrecked early in a storm. Some of his men tried to

► A Portuguese map of the 16th century, showing South America and the Strait of Magellan. (Far right). The strait in good weather – a shortcut to the Pacific.

mutiny. One ship turned back in fear. Magellan faced terrifying seas at the tip of South America. Luckily, he discovered a channel that led into the Pacific, now called the Strait of Magellan.

Into the Pacific

Food and water ran low as they crossed the huge Pacific Ocean. They had to eat rats, rotten biscuits, and leather. At last they reached the Philippines. Magellan and 40 of his men died fighting the local people as he tried to **convert** them to Christianity. Two ships sailed on. The Portuguese captured one ship. The other finished the three-year voyage with only 18 men – the first to sail around the world.

The dragon who circled the world

The second great explorer to sail around the world was Sir Francis Drake, from England. Queen Elizabeth I hired him to raid Spanish ships carrying gold and silver from Spanish America. In 1569, he saw the Pacific Ocean beyond what is now Panama.

In 1577, the Queen sent Drake around South America to the Asian islands for spices. If Drake could rob a ship or two of its cargo on his way, so much the better.

When storms drove Drake off course, he found another way to pass around the tip of South America. Later, sailing through the Pacific, he captured one ship carrying 20 tons of silver!

Looking for an easy way back to the Atlantic, he went as far north as Canada. There was no way eastwards, so he decided to sail around the world to get home. He brought back millions of pounds worth of Spanish treasure. The Spaniards called him El Draque – the Dragon.

CHAPTER FOUR

EXPLORING THE PACIFIC

Land of the South

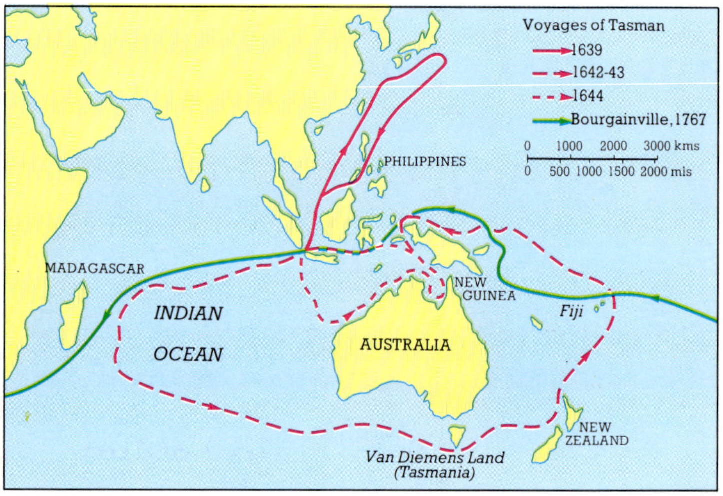

► This map of Australasia shows the routes of the Dutchman Tasman and the Frenchman Bougainville.

In the late 16th century, Europeans believed there was an undiscovered continent in the South Pacific. The Spaniards wanted to find it first. They even named the unseen place Australia, or 'land of the south'.

The Dutch

Willem Jantszoon, a Dutch sailor, first saw Australia in 1606. In 1642, Abel Tasman, another Dutchman, became the first European to sail around Australia. He discovered New

▲ This map of the world drawn in 1595 shows a huge continent that no one had ever seen. Scientists of those days believed that the land was needed there to balance continents in the north.

Zealand, Tasmania, and some other South Pacific islands.

Louis de Bougainville

A French officer, Louis de Bougainville, took scientists along on a Pacific voyage in 1766-69. Many discoveries were made. Jeanne Baré was an expert **botanist** and the first woman to take part in a great voyage of exploration.

◀ When white people first came to Tasmania, they killed many of the Aborigines. Others died from too much drink or disease. These last ones died in the 1860s.

James Cook

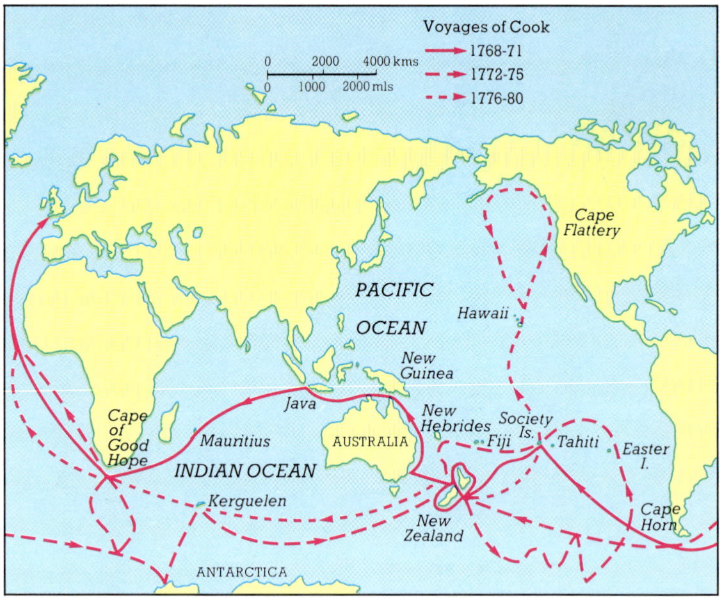

► This map shows the three voyages of Captain Cook.

▲ Cook was a superb sailor and a great leader. He fed his men well to prevent diseases like scurvy.

James Cook, born in 1728, was one of the greatest explorers of the Pacific Ocean. He was a brilliant mathematician and an expert **navigator**. He was interested in making **charts** to show how the planets moved. He also had a secret mission to find a continent south of Australia.

Cook's voyages

Cook made three voyages in the late 1700s. During his first voyage, he drew maps of several islands in the South Pacific, including New Zealand. On his second voyage, he sailed farther south. He did not reach Antarctica, but he did find an icy

◀ Captain Cook's ship, the *Endeavour,* was very strong and measured 30 metres in length.

region of fog and icebergs, where even his sails froze stiff! On his third voyage in 1778, he discovered the Hawaiian Islands. He sailed north through the Bering Strait, searching for a sea route through North America. When ice stopped him, he returned to Hawaii. There, in a fight over a stolen boat, Hawaiians killed him.

Harrison's clock

Englishman John Harrison invented a clock in 1761 that would keep accurate time at sea. For the first time, sailors could find their ship's position east or west. This is called longitude. They compared the local time with the time in England. Cook used Harrison's clock to make accurate maps.

◀ On Cook's second visit to Hawaii, some local people stole one of his boats. When his men tried to get it back, a fight broke out and the Hawaiians killed Cook.

CHAPTER FIVE

ACROSS THE NEW WORLD

The Northwest Passage

▲ Martin Frobisher was a strong Yorkshireman with a bad temper.

While the Spanish were colonizing Central and South America, the British turned their attention to North America. They were convinced that they could find a sea passage around the top of North America that connected the Atlantic and Pacific Oceans. They called it the Northwest Passage.

Sir Martin Frobisher

In 1576, Martin Frobisher was one of the first people to make a serious search for the Northwest Passage. During his search, he and his men were surrounded by **Inuit** warriors in **kayaks**. Five of Frobisher's men disappeared while exploring, so, in anger, he captured an Inuit and took him back to England. Frobisher made three trips in search of the Northwest Passage, but never found it.

◀ Inuit attacked Frobisher's men as they explored Baffin Island.

▼ Frobisher captured this Inuit man and took him back to England.

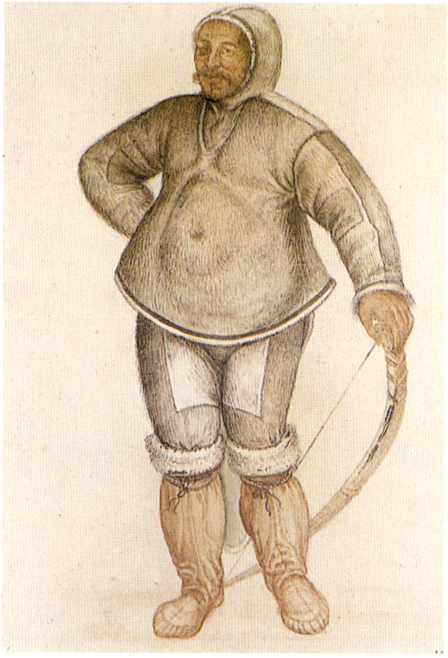

▼ Polar bears present another danger for Arctic explorers.

Henry Hudson

In 1610, Henry Hudson sailed to North America to find the Northwest Passage. When he reached Canada, Hudson spent the winter with his men in a huge bay, now called Hudson's Bay. Later, his men mutinied. They set him adrift in an open boat, leaving him, his son, and seven companions to die.

Going West

The French explored the inland areas of North America, going by canoe. They traded with the Indians. Jacques Cartier was the first Frenchman to explore Canada. He explored the Gulf of St. Lawrence in 1534 and the St. Lawrence River in the next year.

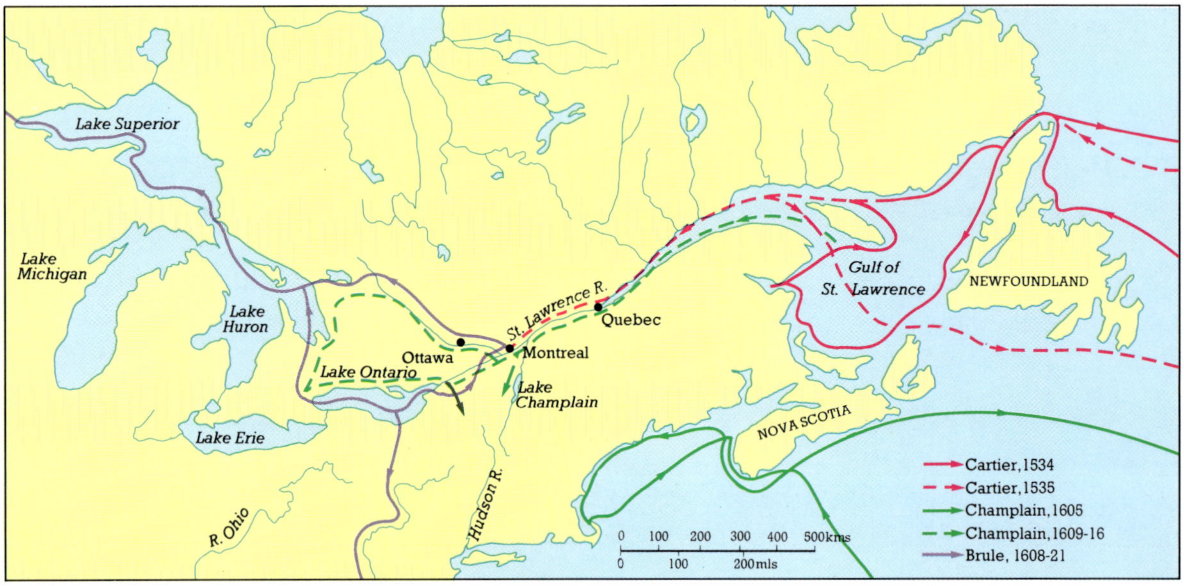

▲ This map shows the routes of the early French explorers in North America.

Later explorers

Sixty years later, Samuel de Champlain, looked for a way across the continent. He explored around Lake Ontario and **founded** a colony in that area. At about the same time, Etienne Brulé explored Lake Ontario, Lake Huron, and Lake Superior. He nearly reached the centre of

the continent. In 1682, Robert de la Salle explored the Mississippi, all the way to the Gulf of Mexico. Alexander MacKenzie, a Scot, explored the great MacKenzie River. He also explored westward from Lake Athabasca. In 1793 he and his men struggled over the Rockies. They were the first to reach the Pacific Ocean overland after a difficult two-month journey.

▲ Early European explorers and settlers traded with the Indians. In exchange for guns, metal tools, and alcoholic drinks, the Indians gave them furs that were valued highly in Europe.

▼ Watched by Indians, Jacques Cartier's 1535 expedition sails westward up the St. Lawrence River.

Breakout from the East

► Frontiersmen lived dangerous lives. They travelled over unknown land and risked being attacked by native Indians and wild animals, like bears.

► Basic items every frontiersman needed to keep warm and safe and for hunting.

By the mid-1700s, the **settlements** on the east coast were crowded. People began moving west.

Daniel Boone

For a hundred years, men had crossed the Appalachian Mountains to hunt. The best known **frontiersman** was Daniel

Boone. He hunted and explored in Kentucky for years. People began to follow him to find new homes.

Lewis and Clark

In 1803 the US bought a vast

◄ Long lines of wagons rolled along trails found by the first explorers of the American West. This wagon train heads across the prairies into the Rocky Mountains.

stretch of land. It needed to be explored. Meriwether Lewis and William Clark were the leaders of the expedition. They set out in 1804 across the mid-western **prairies**. Soon they were in unknown territory, facing the Rocky Mountains that seemed too high to cross. Fortunately, one member of the expedition was married to a **Shoshoni** Indian woman. She guided them through the mountains, and later saved their lives from Indian warriors.

Lewis and Clark and their men went down the Columbia River to the Pacific. They returned safely the next year. Their **expedition** covered 12,000 kms (7,500 miles) in $2\frac{1}{4}$ years.

▼ A frontiersman from the time of Daniel Boone – between 1750-1800.

CHAPTER SIX

EXPLORING ASIA

Across Russia

▲ A portrait of Peter the Great. He was keen to know more about what he called his 'empire'.

Until the 1550s, Siberia was unexplored. In 1581, 1,600 Russian **Cossacks** marched over the Ural Mountains to conquer northern Asia. By 1640, the Russians had crossed Asia and reached the Pacific coast.

Peter the Great

Peter the Great (1672-1725), the Tsar of Russia, sent explorers to Siberia's far east. The most outstanding explorer of this area was Vitus Bering. He sailed north through the 90 km (55 mile) gap between Asia and North America. In 1741, he explored the coast of Alaska. He was shipwrecked on

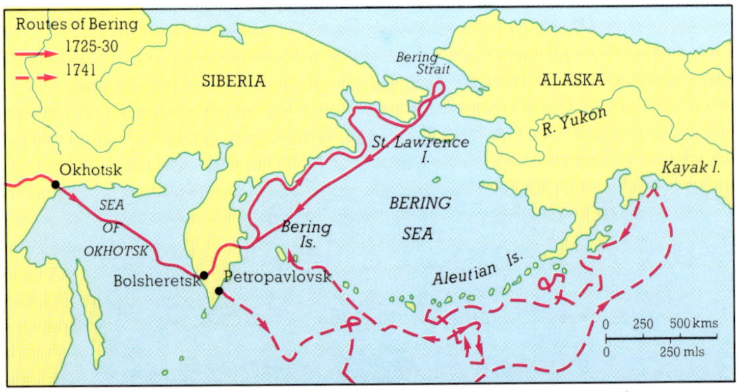

► This map shows the routes Vitus Bering took exploring the coasts of Siberia and Alaska.

barren Bering Island. He and 28 of his men died there of scurvy.

The Tien Shan mountains

The greatest Russian traveller, Nikolai Przhevalsky made five long trips across Mongolia and China. He explored the rugged, unknown Tien Shan mountains of Central Asia in the 1870s. There, Przhevalsky discovered herds of wild horses. They are named after him.

▲ The Tien Shan mountains – a vast barrier between the USSR and China.

▲ The Przhevalsky horse has a woolly coat. This keeps them warm.

The Himalayas

After the Polos, few westerners travelled over the Himalayas to China. In 1661, John Grueber and Albert d'Orville, two **Jesuits**, went to China to set up a European trade route from China to India. They were the first

▲ Mountain climbing became a popular sport in the 19th century.

► The Potala, a great monastery, overlooks the city of Lhasa in Tibet. This was called the Forbidden City because foreigners were not allowed there.

◀ At 8,848 m high, the triangular peak of Everest is the highest in the world (left). But it is almost equalled by other Himalayan giants, like Nuptse (centre) and Lhotse (right).

Europeans to see Lhasa, the capital of Tibet.

Map-making

Travellers usually took regular routes through the Himalayas. But map-makers had to go off these paths. George Everest was the greatest map-maker. Mt. Everest, the world's highest mountain, is named after him.

Did you know?

In 1953, the first men to the top of Mt. Everest were Sir Edmund Hillary and Sherpa Tensing.

Perhaps the greatest explorer of Central Asia was Sven Hedin. He made many journeys and maps of the region. On one journey, between 1894-97, Hedin travelled 19,000 km (12,000 miles) and made 552 pages of maps. Scholars from India, called Pundits, also made maps. Disguised as **pilgrims**, they often explored remote areas.

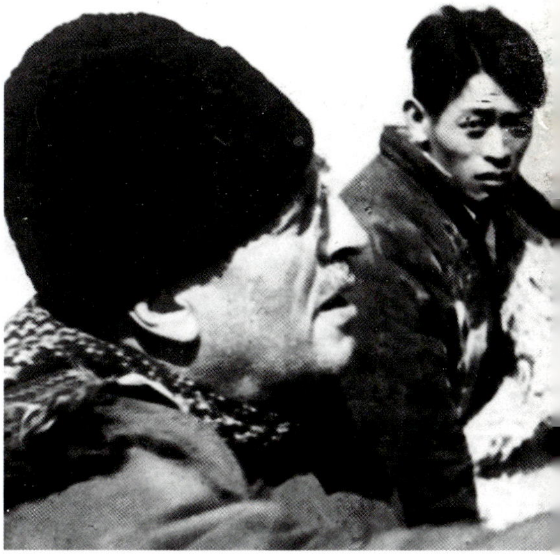

▲ Sven Hedin, the Swedish explorer, spent most of his life travelling in China and India. He is 70 years old in this picture

Arabian Sands

The Arabs knew their own lands beyond the Red Sea. But the Europeans did not. They had to explore Arabia for themselves.

Mecca

Explorers found it difficult to get to the holy city of **Mecca**. There was a harsh desert to cross and only Muslims were allowed to enter the holy city. In 1500 the first European to see Mecca sneaked in with some pilgrims. In 1762 Danish scientists made the first official exploration of Arabia. Unluckily, all but one

► Muhammad, the Prophet of Islam, was born in Mecca – the holiest city in the Muslim world. At the centre is a square building called the Kaaba. Muslims believe it was built by Abraham. Mecca is closed to non-Muslims.

died of disease. Johann Burckhardt, a Swiss, was more successful. He learned Arabic, dressed like an Arab, and then travelled up the Nile. In 1813 he was the first European to see the great rock temple of Abu Simbel. It had statues 18 m (60 feet) tall. The Arabs thought so well of Burckhardt that they declared him Muslim and allowed him to visit Mecca. In the 19th century, Richard Burton visited Mecca, disguised as an Afghan doctor. During World War I, the Arabs rose up against their Turkish rulers. An Englishman, known as Lawrence of Arabia, fought for the Arabs. He explored the Arabian desert and wrote about what he had found.

▲ (Top) The Empty Quarter of southern Arabia is the world's largest sand desert. (Above) Wilfred Thesiger was the last European to cross the Empty Quarter, in 1948-50. The first was Bertram Thomas, in 1930-31.

CHAPTER SEVEN

SOUTH AMERICA

El Dorado

In the 1500s, the Spaniards went to South America to take as much as gold as possible. For over a hundred years, they stole gold and silver from the Indians.

The gilded man

The Spaniards heard about a tribe in Colombia that had an unusual ceremony. Every year, they covered their chief with gold dust that he later washed off in a lake. The Spaniards called this chief El Dorado, meaning 'the

▼ (Inset) The route of Orellana's expedition down the Amazon. (Below) The Amazon runs through the largest rain forest in the world.

gilded man'. Actually, the tribe was small and had little gold.

Exploring the Amazon

After conquering the **Incas** in 1533, the Spaniards began to search for El Dorado. Gonzalo Pizarro and Francisco de Orellana marched 80 men down from the Andes into the **tropical** rain forest. After a month, they could find no food except frogs and snakes. Orellana took 50 men in a boat to search for food. The current swept them down the Amazon river. After fighting hostile tribes, they reached the Atlantic. They travelled almost 5,000 kms and were the first Europeans to cross South America.

▲ The Incas used gold for ornaments, not for money. This is a gold death mask made in Peru around AD 1200.

▼ Lake Guatavita, in Colombia, where the chief, known as El Dorado, washed gold dust from his body. The Orellana expedition never found the tribe.

Into the Amazon

▼ The Humboldt Current sweeps north from Antarctica.

► Chimborazo, a snow-capped volcano in the Andes. Humboldt was the first to climb it in 1802. He reached a height of 5,878 metres, setting a record that was not broken for 30 years.

The Amazon basin explorers were mostly scientists. The first, Frenchman Charles-Marie de la Condamine, examined the area in 1743. He found a great number of plants and animals to study in the Amazon region.

Alexander von Humboldt
The greatest scientist-explorer was the German, Alexander von Humboldt. In 1799, he and French botanist Aimé Bonpland followed the Orinoco River. They found many strange creatures – **piranhas**, stingrays, electric eels, and freshwater dolphins. They also saw the Casiquiare Canal, a natural waterway that connects the Orinoco to the Amazon. Later, in the Andes, they climbed the volcano Chimborazo, 6,272 m high. Humboldt was 300 metres

from the top but the height made him sick. And there was a **ravine** that he could not cross. He had to turn back.

The Humboldt Current

Humboldt discovered why there was a desert in Peru. The desert is close to the Equator. Nearby is the Pacific Ocean, where a **current** (the Humboldt current) from Antarctica keeps the water very cold. This mixture of heat on the land and cold in the sea stops rain from falling.

▲ (Above) The explorer-scientist Humboldt (standing) at a camp high in the Andes. (Below) A portrait of Alexander von Humboldt. ▼

Amazon Life

▲ Henry Bates was attacked by a flock of birds when he captured a toucan for his animal collection.

The Amazon Basin

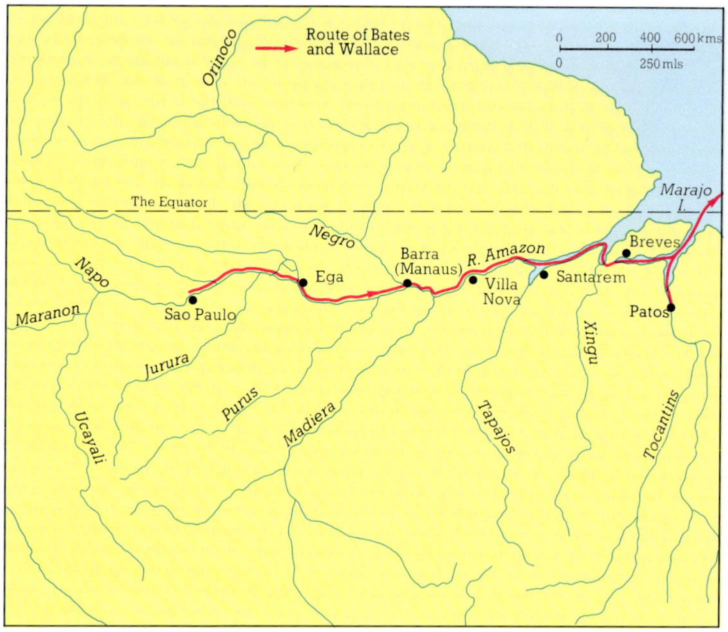

In 1848, Henry Bates and Alfred Wallace, two English scientists, studied Amazon life to learn how different plants and animals **evolved**.

Collecting species

In several years, Bates collected about 14,000 different kinds of insects, over half of them had never been recorded. But Wallace lost his own collection in a fire on the ship. Hamilton Rice, from the US, tried to find the **source** of the Orinoco River, but hostile tribes drove him away. A Brazilian, Candido Rondon, made many trips to meet Indian tribes. He once travelled with former US

▲ Wildlife of the Amazon.

President Theodore Roosevelt. Roosevelt said the Amazon was a 'green hell'.

Mapping the Amazon

The best known Amazon explorer was Percy Fawcett. For years he made maps of new areas. In 1925, he and his son went to search for an ancient lost city. They vanished without a trace. Indians probably killed them.

▼ Col. Percy Fawcett and his son disappeared in the Amazon in 1925.

CHAPTER EIGHT

AFRICA

The Sahara

At the end of the 18th century, the inland areas of Africa were still unknown to Europeans. British explorers went there to look for wealth, scientific information, and new lands. First they wanted to find Timbuktu, visited 400 years earlier by Ibn Battuta. They also wanted to find where the River Niger began.

Timbuktu

In 1824, a British Major, Alexander Laing, set out to find Timbuktu. It took him over a year, and Tuareg tribesmen nearly killed him. Laing was the first European to cross the Sahara Desert from north to south and enter Timbuktu. He never lived to describe this famous city. His guide killed him soon after he left it. René Caillie, a Frenchman, was the first European to describe Timbuktu. He reached the city in 1828.

The River Niger

In 1795, Mungo Park, a 24-year-old Scottish doctor, set out to map

▼ Mungo Park mapped the River Niger.

the River Niger. He survived many adventures, including four months in prison. He travelled 500 kms (300 miles) and discovered that the Niger flowed east. In 1805, he returned with 40 Europeans to find where it ran out into the sea. They set out from the River Gambia, but only a few lived to reach the Niger. The rest, including Park, died before reaching the river's mouth.

In 1822, three men travelled to Africa's Lake Chad. They were the first Europeans to see it. One man died, but Dixon Denham and Hugh Clapperton brought back amazing reports of African kingdoms south of the Sahara.

▲ Timbuktu, once a rich trade city, is on the southern edge of the Sahara Desert. The Tuareg, like the man below, and the Arabs have been trading here for centuries.

The Nile

▶ This map shows three expeditions to find the source of the Nile.

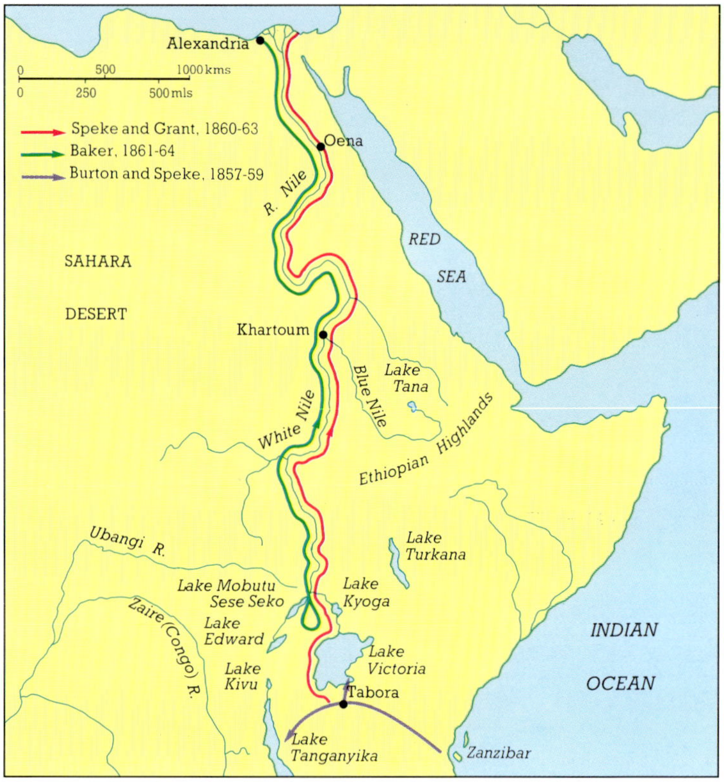

▲ Richard Burton once disguised himself as an Afghan, so he could enter Mecca, the holiest Muslim city.

By the mid-19th century, people still did not know where the source of the River Nile was. It seemed such a mystery. Some said it rose between 'the Mountains of the Moon'. The British Royal Geographical Society sent an expedition in 1856. The leader was Richard Burton. He was an army officer who could speak 25 different languages.

Lake Victoria

In 1857, Burton and John Speke, discovered Lake Tanganyika. Both men became sick, but Speke was strong enough to go on. He

travelled north to find a great lake, Lake Victoria. Speke was sure this was the Nile's source. He returned home ahead of Burton and broke the news. Speke soon organized another expedition, and James Grant joined him. They found where one branch of the Nile flows out of Lake Victoria. They missed finding out that the river also flowed through Lake Albert. Later, they met Samuel Baker and his wife. They were also searching for the Nile's source. The Bakers reached Lake Albert and Murchison Falls in 1864.

▲ The Murchison Falls, where the River Nile flows out of Lake Albert.

▼ Up until the 19th century people believed that the source of the River Nile lay somewhere near Mount Kilimanjaro in Tanzania.

Missionary Explorers

► David Livingstone and Henry Morton Stanley explored and mapped much of central Africa.

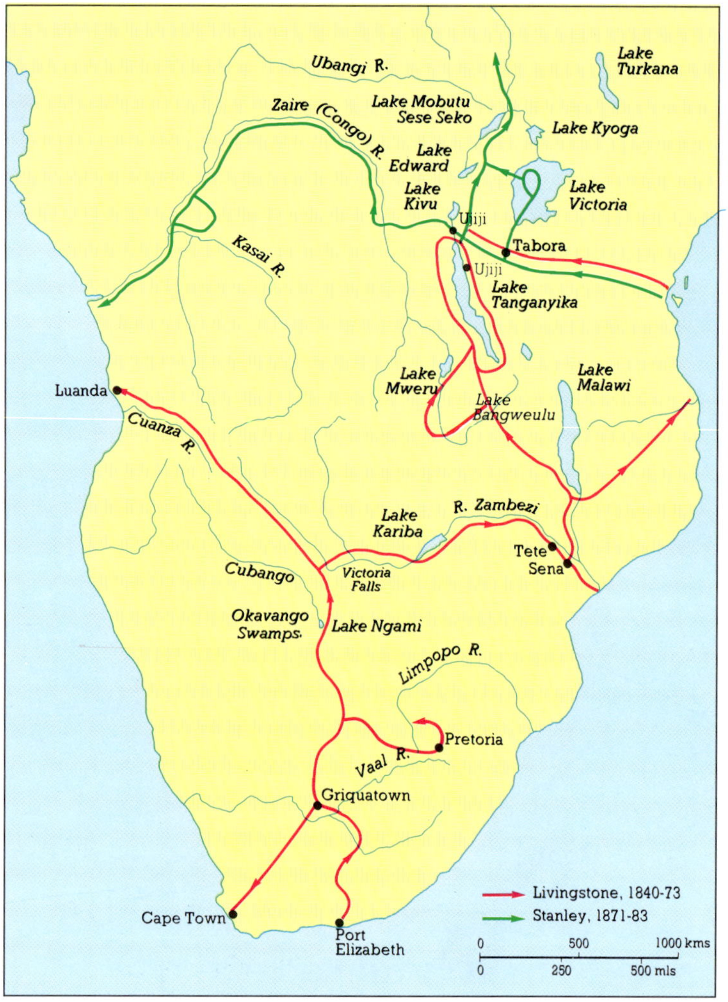

▼ Livingstone explored the River Zambezi in 1855-56. He reported that it was calm. But at that time he had not seen the fierce Quebrabasa rapids.

David Livingstone is a very famous explorer. In 1841 he went to South Africa as a **missionary**. He was one of the first to cross the Kalahari desert. He found Lake Ngami. Next, he crossed Africa from coast to coast, searching for a good trade route. In 1858, he led a British expedition up the Zambezi River, but dangerous **rapids** blocked his way. Later, in 1866, he began searching for the sources of the Nile and Congo rivers. He ran out of money and supplies, and fell ill on the shore of Lake Tanganyika. When he did not return, people thought he was lost or dead.

Henry Morton Stanley

Just then Henry Morton Stanley, a US news reporter, arrived with supplies. Stanley spoke those famous words, 'Dr. Livingstone, I presume?' Livingstone recovered and went on trying to find the 'mountains of the moon'. In 1873 he fell ill again and died. Stanley led several more expeditions. He explored more of central Africa by travelling along the River Congo.

▼ Sailing up the Zambezi in his boat, Livingstone found the dangerous rapids he missed earlier.

▼ On a later expedition, Livingstone fell ill. His food and medicine had been stolen. Just in time, Stanley reached him with fresh supplies.

CHAPTER NINE

INLAND AUSTRALIA

Across the Divide

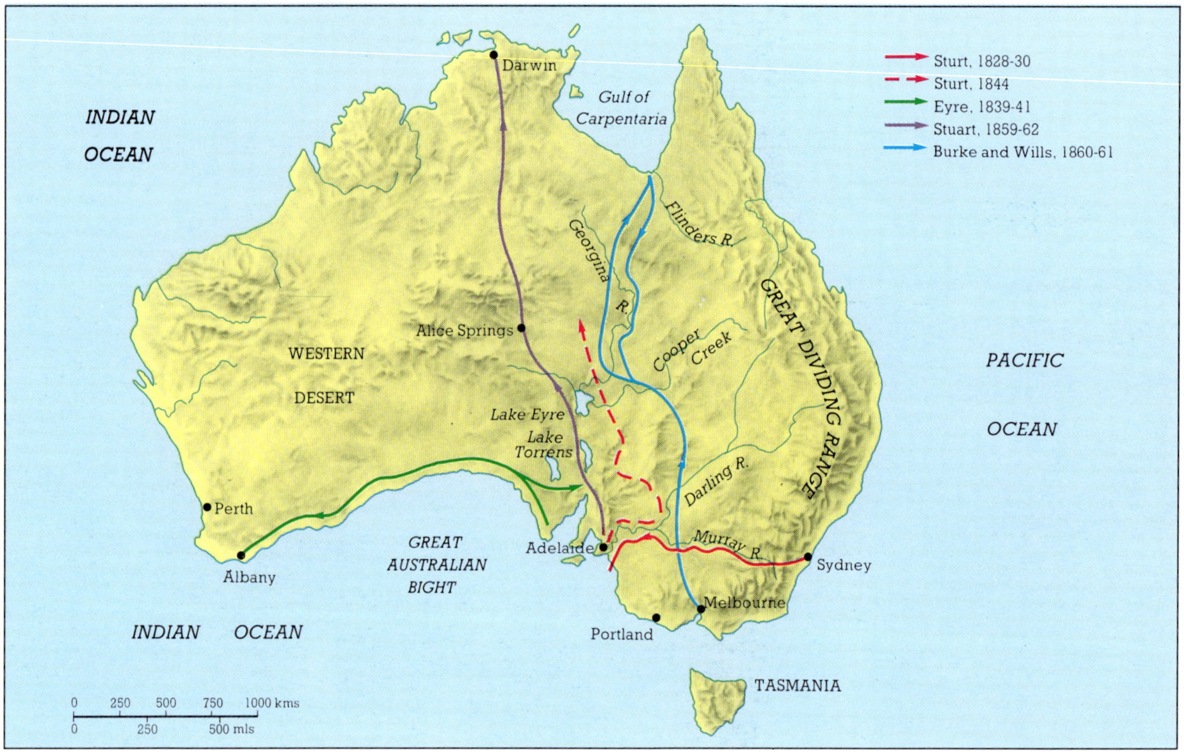

▲ The routes of the main explorers of Australia's outback, or inland.

For **decades** after the British first settled in Australia, few crossed the Great Dividing Range of mountains along the eastern shore. Only the Aborigines lived in the outback – inland Australia.

Mapping inland

In 1829, Charles Sturt and six others explored down the

Murrumbidgee and Murray rivers to the southern coast. Then they rowed back against the current for nearly 1,600 km (1,000 miles). They made reports of good land and many people started moving west. About ten years later, Edward Eyre left Adelaide to explore northward. When he reached desert areas, he turned west instead. He found that in 1,600 kms (1,000 miles) of the south desert coast there were no rivers. Two guides killed his companion and stole the supplies. Eyre and one faithful Aborigine, Wylie, came across a French ship and were given food. They went on until they reached Albany.

▲ The Darling River and others like it helped explorers reach inland Australia.

◀ These cliffs in the Great Dividing Range, 150 metres high, show why it was a major barrier to explorers.

▼ Edward Eyre and the Aborigine, Wylie, survived the 1840 exploration of the south coast.

The Simpson Desert

► Charles Sturt starting off on his journey of 1844. He hoped to find a great inland sea, but found only seas of grass, and sand and rock.

▼ Robert Burke was brave, but his bad temper made him unpopular.

Charles Sturt believed there was an inland lake in Australia. In 1844 he led an expedition to find it. The men spent months in desert country. Then they entered the Simpson Desert, a huge wasteland of red rock and sand. Sturt turned back.

The Telegraph Race

In 1859, the government of

Australia decided to link north and south by **telegraph**. It offered a prize of £2,500 to the first person who could make the crossing. Two rival teams set out. John Stuart led one team. They went farther north than any European had gone before. They passed Alice Springs and a

mountain that was later named after Stuart. When he ran out of food, he had to turn back. He was only 500 kms (300 miles) from the north coast. Two years later, he made it all the way. Robert Burke led the second team, using camels to help them. He split his men into two groups, one to wait for supplies to catch up, the other to hurry north. Burke and William Wills made a final dash and completed the crossing from south to north. They had planned to meet up with the others back at Cooper's Creek. But they could not find each other. All died of starvation but John King — a walking skeleton kept alive by Aborigines.

▲ Cooper's Creek was the meeting place for Burke and his men. Most of them died in the deserts near here.

▼ Here is a camel caravan like the one Burke used for his expedition. He was the first to bring these animals into Australia. Camels travel better in deserts than horses.

CHAPTER TEN

THE ENDS OF THE EARTH

The North

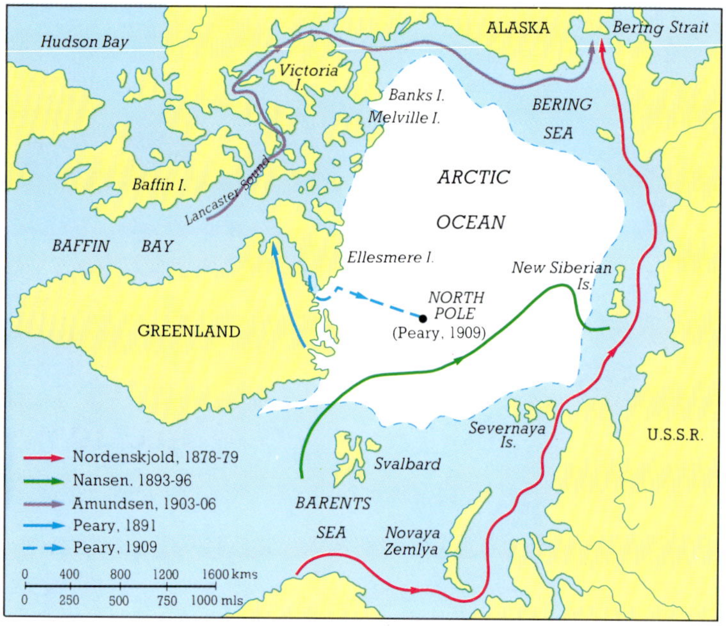

► This map shows the routes of the major Arctic expeditions.

First to the Pole

Robert Peary of the United States was the first person to reach the North Pole in 1909.

▼ An Inuit family, dressed warmly to survive the severe cold of the far north.

For centuries, people have wondered about the remote icy regions of the far north. In the 19th century, several British explorers travelled north of Canada. They could not find the Northwest Passage that would connect the Pacific and Atlantic oceans.

Discovering Magnetic North

In 1829, John Ross led the Arctic

◀ Wally Herbert and his men were the first to cross the polar ice cap.

Nansen

Nansen Fridtjof Nansen from Norway designed a ship that would slip up out of the water when ice closed in. In 1893, after sailing north, Nansen let his ship freeze in. He then went on with sleds and kayaks. Nansen came within 386 kms (240 miles) of the Pole.

expedition that found the **Magnetic North Pole**. He had to abandon his damaged ship and live in a small makeshift house during the Arctic winter. Luckily, a whaling ship rescued them. Sir John Franklin led a less fortunate expedition in 1845. His ship became frozen in ice and he died. Some of his men tried to walk away on the ice, but they too met with a chilly death. Baron Nils Nordenskjold, a Swedish explorer, travelled north of Siberia and found the Northeast Passage in 1878-79. The Northwest Passage was finally navigated in 1903-06 by Roald Amundsen, from Norway.

▼ Fridtjof Nansen was a great explorer and a brilliant scentist. He also drew fine illustrations of his travels.

The South

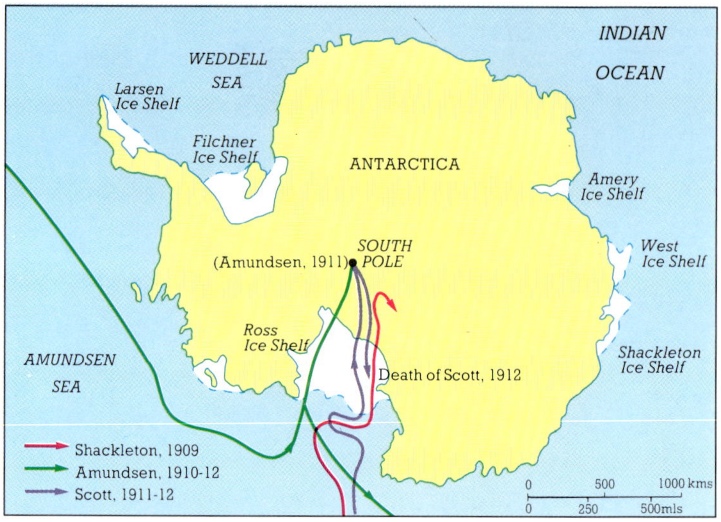

▶ The main routes in search of the South Pole.

▲ Robert Scott writes in his diary before setting out for the South Pole.

Antarctica was the last continent to be explored. Explorers raced to be first to the South Pole.

The Race to the South Pole
In 1908 Ernest Shackleton, a British explorer, discovered the Beardmore Glacier. He almost

▶ In the Antarctic, high winds whip the snow into a fog-like, blinding white out. Bare flesh can freeze in less than a minute.

reached the South Pole. Just 160 kms (100 miles) from the pole he ran short of food and had to turn back. In 1911, two men raced for the pole. Roald Amundsen, a Norwegian, used Arctic sledge dogs called huskies. British expedition leader Robert Scott had ponies and motorized sledges. The sledges soon broke down. The ponies could not survive the cold. For four weeks, Scott and his men hauled their supplies on foot. Then Scott took four men and hurried the remaining 286 kms (178 miles) to the pole. When they arrived they found Amundsen had been there 34 days earlier, on 14 December, 1911. With his dogs, he had made the trip in seven weeks. Scott and his four men died on the return journey.

▲ The Beardmore Glacier.

▼ Here is Shackleton's well-stocked base hut.

The bitter end

From the South Pole, Scott and his men started back to their base camp, 300 kms (200 miles) away. They were running out of food and were exhausted. One died on the Beardmore Glacier. Another man aware that food was running out, wandered away. The other three died 12 days later, only 18 kms (11 miles) from food and shelter.

◀ The Norwegian flag is raised over the South Pole.

The Last Unknown

► Ernest Shackleton had his ship, *Endurance,* locked in ice for nine months, and then it sank.

▼ The type of clothing modern explorers need to survive in the Arctic and Antarctic.

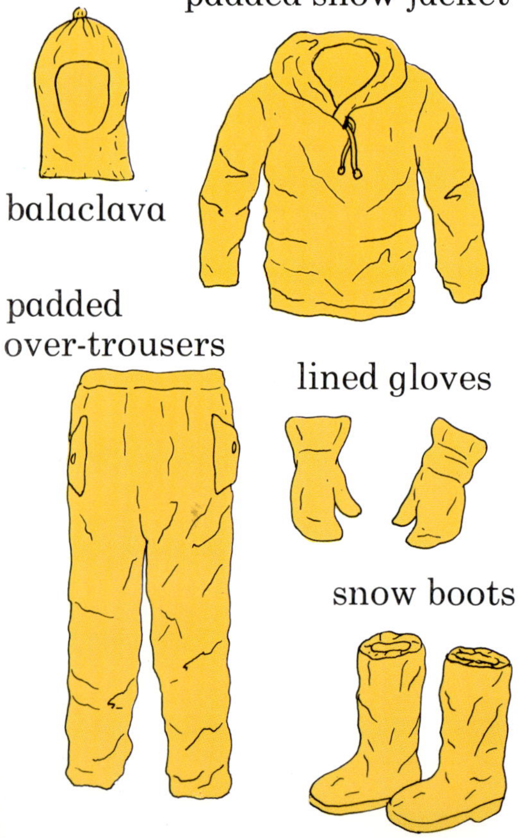

In 1915, Ernest Shackleton made one of the most heroic journeys in Antarctica. His ship froze in the ice and later sank. He and his 28 crewmen camped for four months on the ice until it broke up. They rowed to a small island. Then Shackleton and five men sailed in a small boat 1,400 kms (870 miles) to an island whaling station for help. All of his men were saved.

Mapping and photographing
Today, our interest in Antarctica

is scientific. In 1946, the US sent a crew to map and photograph over half the coast. In 1957, a British team crossed Antarctica in snow-mobiles. They found that the **icecap** averages 2.5 kms (1.5 miles) thick. If it melted, it would be as much water as the Atlantic Ocean!

The 12 Nation Treaty

In 1959, 12 nations signed a treaty, promising not to claim any more Antarctic land and to use the area only for peaceful research.

▲ Ice-breakers like this make modern Antarctic research safer.

Frontiers of the Future

Today, it is easier and safer to explore our world. Now **satellites** can photograph the Earth from unlimited heights, and submersibles can reach the deepest ocean floors.

New challenges

Many challenges still remain for curious and brave explorers. For example, the deepest known cave is in France. It goes down 1,120 metres (3,872 feet). The Mammoth Cave, in Kentucky USA, is the longest, stretching 300 kms (186

▲ Scientists exploring the mysteries of the world's ocean depths. This submersible craft can withstand the great pressure of water near the ocean floor.

► Space exploration is the next great challenge for humans. Here scientists on the Moon gather rock samples.

miles). Miles of caves wait for exploration. There are also many discoveries to be made in the tropical rain forests. The Amazon holds unknown tribes, animals not yet recorded, and plants that may be valuable to humans. Space exploration is expensive and risky. A single mistake can destroy the mission. But the knowledge gained is worth the risk for the astronauts, who in the future will travel farther into unknown space.

▲ Chris Bonington, a mountaineer, in the Himalayas, using a computer to record his notes.

▼ This man is pot-holing in the Pyrenees, in France. Cave exploring is exciting but very dangerous.

Glossary

Botanist: someone who studies plants.

Charts: this is a word to describe special maps. They not only show where objects are but also what goes on around them. For example, charts of the stars show their yearly movements.

Colony: when a group of people move to a new part of the world and make their homes there, this place is called a colony.

Compass: an instrument that contains a floating magnetic needle that always points to the magnetic north. It is used in finding the direction.

Continent: a large area of land made of many countries. There are seven on Earth. These are Europe, Asia, North America, South America, Australasia, Africa and Antarctica.

Convert: to change or turn from one idea or belief to another. For example, Christians try to convert non-Christians to their religion.

Cossacks: people who came from south-eastern Russia, known for their great skill riding horses. They were also great fighters.

Current: this is a word used to describe the flow of water in the sea.

Decade: the word used to describe ten years. Ten decades is a century (100 years).

Equator: an imaginary circle around the Earth, lying halfway between the North and South Poles.

Evolve: to change slowly through many generations over millions of years from a simple plant or animal to a more complex life form.

Expedition: this is a journey made with some kind of purpose. For example, to explore unknown lands, to find valuable things (like gold or silk) or to take over other lands.

Fleet: a group of ships that sail together.

Found: to start and set something up. For example, a city is founded and so is a club.

Frontiersman: a person who explores and hunts in regions unknown to other people. When Europeans started to explore North America, for example, the frontiersmen went ahead of other people to find good paths, fresh water and food.

Great Khan: this was the title given to the medieval emperors of central Asia.

Icecap: a covering of ice over a rounded area, like a hill or mountain.

Inuit: a member of the peoples who live in Canada and Greenland, once known as Eskimos.

Jesuit: a monk who is Roman Catholic and belongs to the Society of Jesus.

Kayak: a canoe, first used by the Inuit of North America and Greenland.

Magnetic North Pole: the place on the Earth where all compasses point to. It has a pulling force for a type of metal called a lodestone. This is the metal that is used in a compass.

Mecca: a city in Saudi Arabia, where Muhammad, the Prophet of Islam, was born. It is a holy place where many Muslims go to.

Missionary: someone who actively tries to change people to his or her religion.

Mongols: peoples who were ruled by Genghis Khan. They lived in central Asia.

Muslim: someone who is a follower of the faith of Islam, proclaimed by the Prophet Muhammad.

Mutiny: a revolt against those who are in charge. The word is most often used for a revolt in the army or navy.

Navigator: someone who can find the

way by using the stars or instruments such as a compass.

Pharaoh: the title given to a king in ancient Egypt.

Pilgrims: people who travel to holy places to worship.

Piranha: a ferocious fish that lives in rivers in South America. It has strong jaws and razor sharp teeth and can kill cattle or human beings.

Prairies: huge, flat stretches of grassland that have no trees.

Rapids: this is a word used to describe the part of a river that flows very fast. The river is usually going steeply down hill and is full of rocks that make its path dangerous to boats.

Ravine: a deep and narrow valley with extremely steep sides cut into a hillside.

Satellite: something that goes round a larger object. This might be something natural, like the Earth's Moon or it might be man-made like a weather satellite.

Settlement: a plot of land where a group of people settle and live.

Shoshoni: a North American Indian tribe.

Source: the place where a river begins. It is usually up in hills or mountains.

Telegraph: a method of sending messages using electric signals sent through wires.

Tropical: a word used to describe very hot and wet areas of the Earth.

Index

A number in **bold** shows the entry is illustrated on that page. The same page often has writing about the entry too.